1/69

WATCH ANIMALS GROW

Piglets

by Colleen Sexton

BLASTOFF! READERS

BELLWETHER MEDIA · MINNEAPOLIS, MN

Note to Librarians, Teachers, and Parents:

Blastoff! Readers are carefully developed by literacy experts and combine standards-based content with developmentally appropriate text.

Level 1 provides the most support through repetition of high-frequency words, light text, predictable sentence patterns, and strong visual support.

Level 2 offers early readers a bit more challenge through varied simple sentences, increased text load, and less repetition of high-frequency words.

Level 3 advances early-fluent readers toward fluency through increased text and concept load, less reliance on visuals, longer sentences, and more literary language.

Level 4 builds reading stamina by providing more text per page, increased use of punctuation, greater variation in sentence patterns, and increasingly challenging vocabulary.

Level 5 encourages children to move from "learning to read" to "reading to learn" by providing even more text, varied writing styles, and less familiar topics.

Whichever book is right for your reader, Blastoff! Readers are the perfect books to build confidence and encourage a love of reading that will last a lifetime!

3 1561 00220 2020

This edition first published in 2008 by Bellwether Media.

No part of this publication may be reproduced in whole or in part without written permission of the publisher. For information regarding permission, write to Bellwether Media Inc., Attention: Permissions Department, Post Office Box 19349, Minneapolis, MN 55419.

Library of Congress Cataloging-in-Publication Data
Sexton, Colleen A., 1967–
  Piglets / by Colleen Sexton.
    p. cm. — (Blastoff! readers. Watch animals grow)
Summary: "A basic introduction to piglets. Simple text and full color photographs. Developed by literacy experts for students in kindergarten through third grade"—Provided by publisher.
  Includes bibliographical references and index.
  ISBN-13: 978-1-60014-169-0 (hardcover : alk. paper)
  ISBN-10: 1-60014-169-2 (hardcover : alk. paper)
  1. Piglets—Juvenile literature. I. Title.

SF395.5.S49 2008
636.4'07—dc22   2007040274

Contents

A mother pig
has piglets.
Newborn piglets
are very small.

Piglets stay close to their mother. They live together on a farm.

Piglets drink
milk from
their mother.
Milk helps them
grow strong.

Soon farmers
start to feed
piglets **grain**.

11

A piglet has a **snout**. A piglet uses its snout to sniff the ground for food.

Piglets play.
Sometimes they
chase and bite
each other.

Piglets roll in mud
to keep cool.

Piglets sleep
most of the time.
Sleeping helps
them grow.

Piglets grow up fast. Soon they may have piglets of their own!

Glossary

grain—small, hard seeds that come from wheat, rice, corn and other plants

snout—the long nose and jaws of an animal

To Learn More

AT THE LIBRARY

Older, Jules. *Pig*. Watertown, Mass.: Charlesbridge, 2004.

Powell, Jillian. *From Piglet to Pig*. Austin, Tex.: Raintree, 2001.

Stone, Lynn. *Pigs Have Piglets*. Minneapolis, Minn.: Compass Point Books, 2000.

ON THE WEB

Learning more about piglets is as easy as 1, 2, 3.

1. Go to www.factsurfer.com

2. Enter "piglets" into search box.

3. Click the "Surf" button and you will see a list of related web sites.

With factsurfer.com, finding more information is just a click away.

Index

The images in this book are reproduced through the courtesy of: Jorgen Larsson/Masterfile, front cover; Kathy deWitt/Alamy, p. 5; Petr Masek, p. 7; Kevin R. Williams, p. 9; Peter Cade/Getty Images, p. 11; Dirk V. Mallinckrodt/Alamy, p. 13; Andy Sacks/Getty Images, p. 15; Scott Slattery , p. 17; Thorsten Milse/Getty Images, p. 19; ARCO/C. Steimer/Age fotostock, p. 21.